Famous Artists

Get to Know

Georgia O'Keeffe

Charlotte Taylor

Enslow Publishing
101 W. 23rd Street
Suite 240
New York, NY 10011
USA

enslow.com

Published in 2016 by Enslow Publishing, LLC
101 W. 23rd Street, Suite 240, New York, NY 10011

Library of Congress Cataloging-in-Publication Data
Taylor, Charlotte, 1978- author.
 Get to know Georgia O'Keeffe / Charlotte Taylor.
     pages cm. — (Famous artists)
 Includes bibliographical references and index.
 Summary: "Describes the life and work of artist Georgia O'Keeffe"—Provided by publisher.
 ISBN 978-0-7660-7226-8 (library bound)
 ISBN 978-0-7660-7224-4 (pbk)
 ISBN 978-0-7660-7225-1 (6 pk)
1. O'Keeffe, Georgia, 1887-1986—Juvenile literature. 2. Painters—United States—Biography—Juvenile literature.
3. Women painters—United States—Biography—Juvenile literature. I. Title.
 ND237.O5T39 2016
 759.13—dc23
 [B]
                                        2015026941
Printed in the United States of America

Portions of this book originally appeared in *Georgia O'Keeffe: The Life of an Artist* by Ray Spangenburg & Kit Moser.

Contents

Only One (1959, Smithsonian American Art Museum, Washington, DC).
O'Keeffe loved the view from an airplane. She especially liked how the rivers
looked from that height. In 1959, she painted many pictures that were
inspired by this view.

Chapter 1

Young Georgia

Georgia O'Keeffe started painting at a time when women did not get the same chances as men. In the early 1900s, women in the United States did not even have the right to vote. In the art world, almost all the serious artists were men. But O'Keeffe did not let that stop her.

O'Keeffe's paintings were not always pictures of objects or people. She used shapes, form, and color to paint ideas and feelings. She was part of a new group of artists called modernists. Some people thought the new art was exciting. Other people thought it was silly. O'Keeffe didn't care. She knew what she wanted to paint. She did it, and she did it well. Today, people all over the world still get a special feeling from her paintings.

Life on the Farm

Georgia Totto O'Keeffe was born on November 15, 1887. She began life on a dairy farm near Sun Prairie, Wisconsin. People from many different parts of the world came there to find a better life. Georgia's grandparents were among them.

Georgia's father, Frank O'Keeffe, was a handsome Irish-American and a successful farmer and feed-store owner. His family had left Ireland to escape the potato famine, when many people in that country were starving to death. They hoped to find better luck farming on the plains of Wisconsin. Georgia's mother was Ida Totto, the daughter of a Hungarian count. Her father, George Totto, had left his home to escape war.

The Tottos and O'Keeffes became neighbors in Wisconsin. Both families worked hard, and their farms did well. Frank and Ida grew up near each other. Both loved the land. When they married, they began their family on the Totto farm. They had seven children.

Georgia was the second child and the oldest girl among the seven. She grew up feeling that she was in charge of the younger children. She worked hard on the farm. Farm girls usually helped with washing, ironing, and baking. They also had chores to do outdoors. After chores were done, Georgia spent a lot of time alone. She liked the outdoors. The big hay barn across the fields became a symbol of her childhood.

Georgia grew up on a farm in Wisconsin. When she was a teenager, her family moved to Virginia. The farm family did not fit in well.

Untitled (1903/1905, Georgia O'Keeffe Museum, Santa Fe, NM). This image of a teapot and flowers is an early example of what would make Georgia O'Keeffe's paintings famous.

Georgia Makes Up Her Mind

Georgia always felt she was different from other children. "From the time I was small," she later recalled, "I was always doing things other people don't do."

Georgia had made up her mind in the eighth grade. When a school friend asked her what she planned to do when she grew up, she responded boldly, "I'm going to be an artist."

In Sun Prairie, the O'Keeffe children attended a small school. Ida O'Keeffe wanted a better education for her children. So in 1901, Georgia went to the Sacred Heart Academy in the nearby city of Madison. There, she received formal art classes for the first time.

In 1902, Georgia's family made a big change. The winters in Wisconsin were cold and windy. Frank O'Keeffe thought warmer winters would be better for his family's health. He sold the farm and moved his family to Williamsburg, Virginia.

Georgia and her brother Francis stayed behind in Wisconsin and lived with an aunt. They went to the big public high school in the city.

One day, Georgia's art teacher brought a jack-in-the-pulpit flower to class. She showed the students the parts of the flower. She pointed out its deep colors. It was the first time Georgia thought about drawing or painting plants. Many years later, she would become famous for her paintings of plants and flowers.

A Different World

When Georgia joined her family the following year, Virginia was a shock to her. In Wisconsin, women and men had worked together to keep a farm going. Now she lived in the South. Women had a different role. Having nice dresses, good manners, and a soft voice were more important.

Georgia finished high school at the Chatham Episcopal Institute, a boarding school for girls. She lived at the school in Chatham, Virginia. She kept on wearing the sensible clothes she was used to. She didn't let the other girls talk her into frills and ruffles. She thought the other girls were silly. They thought she was awkward and out of place. But they soon found she was also charming and a good friend. Georgia was the only art major to graduate in the class of 1905.

On graduation day, Georgia told her classmates, "I am going to live a different life from you girls. I am going to give up everything for my art."

Georgia never learned to dress or act like her classmates in Virginia. She wore plain clothes and kept her hair back in a ponytail. The other girls wore dresses and wore their hair in ringlets.

Chapter 2

Becoming an Artist

O'Keeffe worked hard at her studies. She was trying to figure out what kind of artist she wanted to be. In the fall of 1905, she went to study at the Art Institute of Chicago. Her studies there were interrupted when she got typhoid fever, a serious illness. Two years later, she attended the Art Students League in New York City.

O'Keeffe knew that New York was an important center for art. There, she studied under the famous artist William Merritt Chase. He told his students not to get stuck doing only one type of art. "Take the best from everything," he said.

O'Keeffe did well in class. She received a scholarship for her work. Yet her classmates did not take her seriously. After all, she was a woman, and most of them were men. They thought she was not a serious artist. One young man said to her, "I am going to be a great painter, and you will probably end up teaching painting in some girls' school."

William Merritt Chase was a well-known art teacher in New York. He taught many famous artists of the nineteenth and twentieth centuries, including Edward Hopper and Georgia O'Keeffe. He was one of the few who would teach women how to paint.

An Unhappy Time

One day, O'Keeffe went with a group of students to visit an art gallery. Some of the latest art from Europe was on exhibit— drawings by the French artist Auguste Rodin. The exhibit hall was called the 291 gallery because it was on the top floor of the building at 291 Fifth Avenue.

The man who owned the gallery was a famous photographer named Alfred Stieglitz. He was also the leader of a group of modernist artists. He and his friends had a lot of influence on art in New York. O'Keeffe watched Stieglitz talk. She thought he was loud and pushy. She was not excited about him or about modernism.

O'Keeffe was not happy with her studies, either. Chase taught his students to copy the great artists of the past. But this was not the art O'Keeffe felt deep inside. She longed to be considered good—even great. But she knew that art, to her, was not a matter of copying old works.

She decided to stop painting. For several years, even the smell of paint and turpentine made her sick!

O'Keeffe went to work drawing fashion advertisements. She drew lace and embroidery as a commercial artist. It was hard work, and she was under a lot of pressure. She was afraid of losing the special feeling she had about art. Then, she got the measles. Her eyes were so hurt by it that she couldn't continue the work.

Without painting in her life, Georgia O'Keeffe felt lost.

O'Keeffe liked the idea that art should show feelings and beauty.

Returning to Art

In the spring of 1911, O'Keeffe began teaching art at her old school, Chatham Institute, in Virginia. O'Keeffe was a good, lively teacher. She found she liked the job. She also began to think about painting again.

Soon, she was taking art classes at the University of Virginia. She took classes from Alon Bement, a student of an artist named Arthur Wesley Dow. They both taught that art's purpose is to show a thought or feeling. Also, all the parts of a painting must work together. They must play in harmony like instruments in a band.

Dow liked the Japanese idea of filling space with beauty. He said an artist needs to develop a sense of beauty. But this sense has to come from inside the artist. O'Keeffe liked this way of looking at art. It meant she had to feel every part of her life— and then put it on canvas.

That fall, O'Keeffe accepted a teaching job in the Amarillo, Texas, school system. It was her first introduction to the American West. She loved the big skies of Texas and the open desert lands.

"It had always seemed to me that the West must be wonderful," O'Keeffe later explained. She liked the openness and beauty of the dry landscape. She thought it was a wonderful, wild world. For the next two years, she taught in her beloved Texas during the school year and at the University of Virginia during the summer.

During these years, O'Keeffe was soaking up experiences. She took classes from Dow at Teachers College at Columbia University in New York. She taught at a women's college in South Carolina.

"Feelings on Paper"

O'Keeffe began work on a special series of drawings. She used charcoal and made curved lines and shaded areas. The drawings were simple but powerful. She was pleased with them. She knew they had come from deep within her. She bundled them up and sent them to Anita Pollitzer, a friend in New York.

When Anita opened the package of drawings, she was excited. She put them under her arm and marched into the 291 gallery. Alfred Stieglitz was there. She showed him the drawings. He looked at them all. "At last," he said. "A woman's feelings on paper." Stieglitz had never really met Georgia, yet he felt he could see who she was from her drawings.

Stieglitz and O'Keeffe began writing letters to each other. Georgia was thrilled that Stieglitz understood what she was trying to express with her drawings.

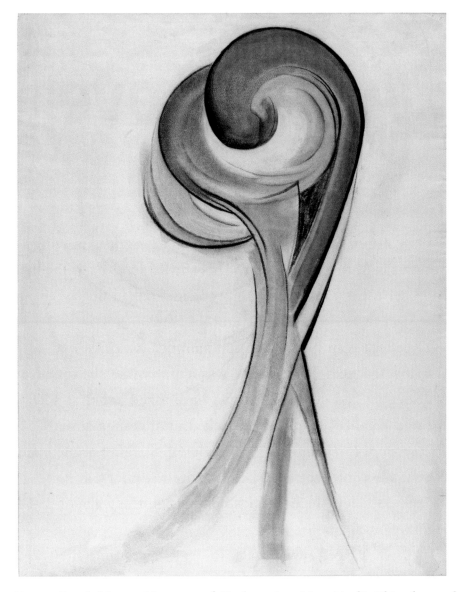

No. 12 Special (1916, Museum of Modern Art, New York). This charcoal drawing was one of O'Keeffe's early works after returning to her life of art.

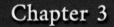
A New Love

In 1916 Alfred Stieglitz hung twelve of O'Keeffe's drawings on the walls of the 291 gallery. This should have been thrilling for O'Keeffe, but there was one problem. He had not asked her permission first. He had not even told her!

O'Keeffe was in New York that summer for classes at Columbia Teachers College. She was angry when she found out what Stieglitz had done. He should have asked her first. She went to the gallery to make him take the drawings down.

They were too beautiful to take down, Stieglitz argued. He said that she could not keep her "children" to herself.

Finally, she left the drawings hanging on the walls of 291. Stieglitz won.

That fall, O'Keeffe went back to Texas. This time she was head of the art department at West Texas State Normal College in Canyon. O'Keeffe loved the canyons and desert hills in this region of the state. The Palo Duro Canyon was like the Grand

Canyon but much smaller. She hiked and camped there. She began painting again.

In 1917, Stieglitz gave O'Keeffe a solo exhibit at the 291 gallery. It was an exciting triumph for her. That same year, O'Keeffe made her first trip to New Mexico. She was stunned by the beauty of the place. She had never seen such wonderful light—not even in Texas.

Free to Paint

The following year, O'Keeffe left Texas and teaching for good. From then on, she would devote her life to her artwork. She moved to New York and spent most of her time painting and drawing.

In 1924, she and Stieglitz married. He was twenty-three years older than she was, but they thought alike about many things. They also had a lot of respect for each other. She enjoyed his praise and encouragement. He loved her

Alfred Stieglitz had a successful art gallery. When he saw O'Keeffe's drawings, he knew she had great talent. He showed her art at his gallery in 1916.

lively ways and bright mind. He also admired her beauty and loved to photograph her.

From the early 1920s until 1929, O'Keeffe spent every summer at Lake George, New York, with Stieglitz's family. The lake was beautiful. The water was clear and cold. Pine forests along the shore provided shade. The buildings at the Stieglitz summer home were country barns and sheds that reminded O'Keeffe of her childhood in Wisconsin. She planted a garden. She painted the trees and the lake. She painted the barns.

She was happy to have the freedom to paint.

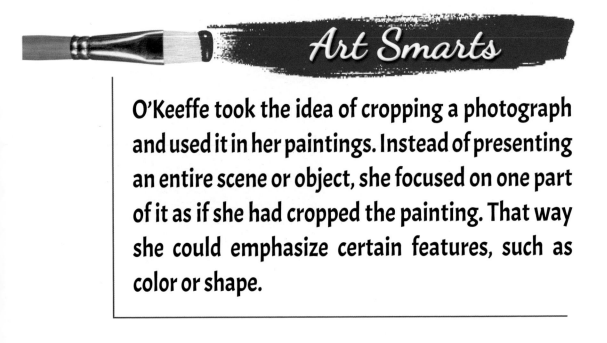

Art Smarts

O'Keeffe took the idea of cropping a photograph and used it in her paintings. Instead of presenting an entire scene or object, she focused on one part of it as if she had cropped the painting. That way she could emphasize certain features, such as color or shape.

Green Oak Leaves (1923, The Newark Museum, Newark, NJ). O'Keeffe was inspired by the lush mountain forests of Lake George, New York. She and Stieglitz spent a lot of time there with family and friends. O'Keeffe said the area made her think of her home in Wisconsin.

Chapter 4

Flowers and Skyscrapers

Artists have always painted flowers. But when O'Keeffe began her flower paintings in 1924, she did it differently.

Her flowers were not small and dainty. They were not pale and gentle like the flowers of other artists. She made her flowers huge and awesome. She made them bright and bold. No one had ever painted flowers this way before. People were amazed.

City Art

A year after they were married, O'Keeffe and Stieglitz moved to the thirtieth floor of the Shelton Hotel in New York. The view of the city from that height was thrilling. O'Keeffe had never lived so high up before.

In the 1920s, some art critics did not like the new buildings in New York. They liked the grace of the cathedrals of Europe. They liked castles on hilltops. The new buildings, they said, looked like

New York Street with Moon (1925, Thyssen-Bornemisza, Madrid, Spain). This oil painting reflects O'Keeffe's love of the new skyscrapers being built when she lived at the Shelton Hotel.

Art Smarts

Many people asked O'Keeffe why she chose to draw flowers so large. She explained that flowers are usually too small to really notice. By painting them big, she wanted to surprise her audience. She wanted to make people stop and pay attention to the flowers.

"boxes with holes in them." They thought artists should paint country scenes. Woods, rolling grasslands, and fields of flowers seemed more worthy of being painted than city streets, tall buildings, traffic, and factories.

O'Keeffe did not agree. She decided to try to paint New York. Later, she wrote, "Of course, I was told that it was an impossible idea—even the men hadn't done too well with it. From my teens on, I had been told that I had crazy notions, so I was accustomed to disagreement and went on with my idea of painting New York." She completed her first painting of the city in 1925.

Purple Petunias (1925, The Newark Museum, Newark, NJ). O'Keeffe began painting flowers in 1924. She chose petunias, calla lilies, and zinnias as her subjects. She became well-known for her larger-than-life flowers.

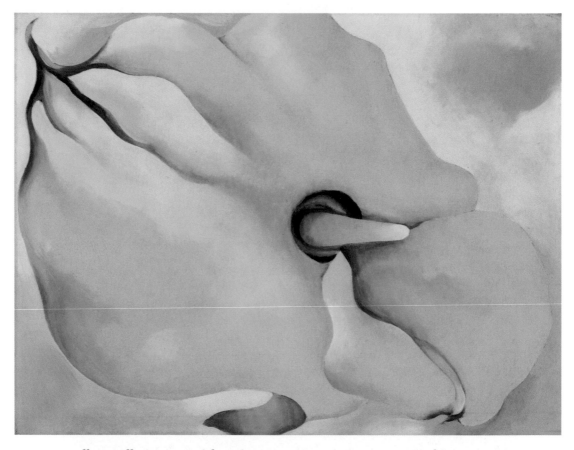

Yellow Calla (1926, Smithsonian American Art Museum, Washington, DC). By the late 1920s, O'Keeffe started to receive recognition for her work.

O'Keeffe's first painting of New York was sold the first afternoon it was on display. "No one ever objected to my painting New York after that," she recalled. She continued painting the city until about 1929.

Chapter 5

New Mexico Summers

Georgia O'Keeffe received a great honor in 1929. The Museum of Modern Art in New York included five of O'Keeffe's works in a special exhibit called Paintings by Nineteen Living Americans.

By this time, O'Keeffe was tired of summers at Lake George. Stieglitz's family and friends were always there. She needed time alone to work and new subjects to paint. She spent that summer painting in New Mexico and the Southwest. After that, she went back there again and again to live and paint. She painted the hills and churches. She painted the bleached bones of the desert. She painted skulls floating over mountains.

It was a big change in her life. Stieglitz did not like to travel. His life and work was in New York City and Lake George. He loved his wife very much, and he missed her when she was gone, but he stayed behind.

O'Keeffe returned to New York each fall to spend the winters with Stieglitz and her New York friends. In 1936, O'Keeffe and

Despite their age difference, O'Keeffe and Stieglitz had a supportive and loving relationship.

O'Keeffe's studio was filled with things she found in the desert of New Mexico.

Stieglitz moved to a penthouse apartment on East Fifty-Fourth Street in New York. But O'Keeffe's heart was in New Mexico.

Ghost Ranch

The next summer, she stayed at a place called Ghost Ranch in New Mexico. The house felt like home to O'Keeffe. A few years later, she bought it.

She became fascinated with the animal bones she found everywhere around Ghost Ranch. She painted lots of skulls and other types of bones. She liked showing bones in new and unusual ways.

In 1945 and 1946, two important retrospective exhibits of her work took place—one at the Chicago Institute of Art and the other at the Museum of Modern Art in New York. O'Keeffe had become an important artist.

One day in July 1946, O'Keeffe received a telegram. Her eighty-two-year-old husband had suffered a stroke. She immediately flew to New York. She stayed by Stieglitz's side in the hospital and was there when he died.

Art Smarts

O'Keeffe began painting animal skulls in the 1930s. On her walks in the desert, she would collect bones that had been bleached white by the sun. For her, they represented the American West. She liked that people were surprised by the bones in her paintings. They did not think this was something a woman should be painting.

Chapter 6

Abiquiu Art

After her husband's death, O'Keeffe stayed in New York for many months. She needed to make arrangements and take care of all of Stieglitz's artwork. In 1949, she returned to New Mexico for good.

She had bought a second house there a few years earlier. This one was a ruin near an old town called Abiquiu. As soon as she had seen it, she had fallen in love with it. The patio and the patio door fascinated her. She painted them many times. For the rest of her life, she would spend every spring and summer at Abiquiu. In fall and winter, she would live in her house at Ghost Ranch.

As always, she loved to be alone. That was when she did her best work.

A Famous Artist

O'Keeffe always remembered the advice of William Merritt Chase to be "artistic in every way." She had become a kind

O'Keeffe liked to spend time in solitude, pondering her life and art.

Visitors to the Art Institute of Chicago view O'Keeffe's *Cow's Skull with Calico Roses* (1931) in 2014. O'Keeffe's work can be seen in museums all over the world, and it continues to grow in popularity.

of celebrity—someone who was famous, admired, and in the news often. In her later years, she always dressed in black for photographs and visitors. She took great care to present herself as someone special.

O'Keeffe received many awards and honors in the 1970s and 1980s. In 1970, the Whitney Museum of American Art held a major retrospective exhibition of O'Keeffe's work. The exhibit also toured Chicago and San Francisco. It was very popular. In 1971, she received the Gold Medal for Painting from the National Institute of Arts and Letters. In 1977, United States President Gerald Ford presented her with the Presidential Medal of Freedom, the highest civilian honor.

Chapter 7

The Light Dims

O'Keeffe was enjoying her success as an artist. Then one day she got some awful news: She was losing her eyesight. The central part of her vision was becoming blurred. Soon, she was almost completely blind. She could no longer see lines, shapes, and colors. She could no longer paint.

That year, she found a new secretary, Virginia Robertson. The two began working on a book titled *Georgia O'Keeffe.* It was about O'Keeffe's life and work. It described how she felt about her paintings. Georgia talked on tape about her memories and thoughts. Virginia listened and typed her words on paper.

A New Friend

Before the book was finished, though, Robertson left. At about this time, a young man stopped by O'Keeffe's gate at Ghost Ranch. Many young artists came to visit her. They admired the dedication she had to her work. They wanted to learn from her.

Near Abiquiu, New Mexico (1941). Ghost Ranch was in the middle of nowhere, which is what O'Keeffe liked about it. The nearest town was a tiny village called Abiquiu, which was seventeen miles away.

This visitor was working at Ghost Ranch. His name was John Hamilton, but everyone called him Juan. He had brown eyes and a big mustache that reminded Georgia of Stieglitz. O'Keeffe found that Hamilton was well educated. He helped her finish her book. It was published in 1976 and became a bestseller.

Hamilton shared many interests with O'Keeffe. He made pottery, and she encouraged him. He gave her an arm to lean on when she walked in the hills. She liked his sense of humor. He was her secretary and close friend in the last years of her life.

White Iris No. 7 (1957, Thyssen-Bornemisz Museum, Madrid, Spain). Although O'Keeffe loved to explore different subjects to paint, she returned to flowers over and over again.

The Georgia O'Keeffe Museum in Santa Fe celebrates the art and life of one of the most distinctive artists of the twentieth century.

Last Years

Over the next ten years, the pair traveled and worked together. Hamilton showed O'Keeffe how to make pottery. She said she liked to try to "make the clay speak." She didn't need her eyes for this art. She could feel the smoothness and shape of the clay with her hands.

In 1984, O'Keeffe became ill and moved from her home in Abiquiu to Santa Fe. She died at Saint Vincent's Hospital in Santa Fe on March 6, 1986. She was ninety-eight years old.

The Georgia O'Keeffe Museum opened in Santa Fe, New Mexico, in July 1997. It is the only museum in the United States that is devoted primarily to the work of a major female artist.

During her long and productive life, O'Keeffe gave the world two thousand paintings, drawings, and sculptures. Today, she is remembered as a great artist. She was also an amazing woman. Perhaps most of all, people think of O'Keeffe as a rare human being—one who knew who she was. And who was always true to herself.

O'Keeffe spent her last years in the desert, where she felt very much at home.

Timeline

1887—Georgia O'Keeffe is born on November 15 in Sun Prairie, Wisconsin.

1901—Enters Sacred Heart Academy in Madison, Wisconsin.

1902—O'Keeffe family moves to Williamsburg, Virginia.

1903–1905—Finishes high school at Chatham Episcopal Institute in Virginia.

1907—Studies at the Art Students League in New York City.

1908—Makes first visit to Alfred Stieglitz's 291 gallery in New York.

1908–1910—Stops painting. Works as a commercial artist in Chicago.

1916—Stieglitz exhibits O'Keeffe's drawings at the 291 gallery in New York.

1917—First solo exhibition opens at 291 gallery in New York.

1923—Stieglitz opens the first annual exhibition of O'Keeffe's work.

1924—Marries Alfred Stieglitz. Begins painting large flowers.

1925—Moves with Stieglitz to New York. Begins cityscapes.

1937—Stays for the first time in house she later buys at Ghost Ranch, New Mexico.

1945—Purchases property near the ancient town of Abiquiu, New Mexico.

1946—Stieglitz dies at age eighty-two.

1949—Moves permanently to New Mexico.

1976—The book *Georgia O'Keeffe* is published and becomes a bestseller.

1977—Receives the Presidential Medal of Freedom, the highest American civilian honor.

1986—Dies March 6 at a hospital in Santa Fe at age ninety-eight.

2014—O'Keeffe's painting *Jimson Weed/White Flower No. 1* sells for more than $44 million.

Words to Know

art critic—A person considered an expert in art who judges art, writes about it, and has a say in how valuable it is.

canvas—A type of heavy cloth stretched over a frame on which artists paint pictures.

civilian—A person who is not in the military, on a police force, or on a firefighting force.

commercial art—Drawings, paintings, and other artwork created to promote or advertise a business.

gallery—A room or building where artwork is displayed and sold.

modernists—A group of artists who painted in new ways; they often painted nonrealistic shapes, objects, or scenes.

on exhibit—On display for people to see. Museums put artists' work on exhibit.

penthouse—An apartment at the top of a building.

retrospective—An art show that displays an artist's past work in honor of a long and successful career.

Learn More

Books

Krull, Kathleen. *Lives of the Artists*: *Masterpieces, Messes (And What the Neighbors Thought)*. New York: Houghton Mifflin Harcourt, 2014.

National Gallery of Art. *An Eye for Art*: *Focusing on Great Artists and Their Work*. Chicago: Chicago Review Press, 2013.

Novesky, Amy. *Georgia in Hawaii*: *When Georgia O'Keeffe Painted What She Pleased*. New York: Houghton Mifflin Harcourt, 2012.

Venezia, Mike. *Georgia O'Keeffe*. New York: Children's Press, 2015.

Websites

The Georgia O'Keeffe Museum
okeeffemuseum.org
Provides biographical information, video, and an online collection of O'Keeffe's work.

Artcyclopedia: Georgia O'Keeffe.
artcyclopedia.com/artists/okeeffe_georgia.html
Includes links to O'Keeffe's paintings online, as well as books and articles about her and her work.

Georgia O'Keeffe
georgia-okeeffe.com
Learn more about O'Keeffe's life, writings, painting styles, and numerous awards and honors.

Index